BEADING WORKSHOP

Welcome to the do-it-yourself beading book that dares to be different. Whether you're a beginner, ready to learn the basics, or an experienced beader, you'll find everything you need to know right here and 102 designs to spark your creativity.

Go far beyond the ordinary and immerse yourself in the fascinating world of making beaded jewelry! The BEADING BASICS on pages 2-9 include a wealth of information on beads and findings. And of course, you'll want to discover the TECHNIQUES AT WORK that make our designs so fresh and original— on pages 10-23, we share those exciting details. Use the INDEX on page 40 to quickly locate a specific technique you want to try. Every creative adventure must start with INSPIRATION. So, beginning on page 24, you can view our extensive showcase of design ideas. Necklaces, bracelets, rings, pins, key fobs—you'll find a wide array of sparkling concepts that will capture your imagination!

LEISURE ARTS, INC.
Maumelle, Arkansas

BEADING BASICS

TOOLS & USAGE

To start, needle- and round-nose jewelry pliers and wire cutters are essential. Add more tools as you go.

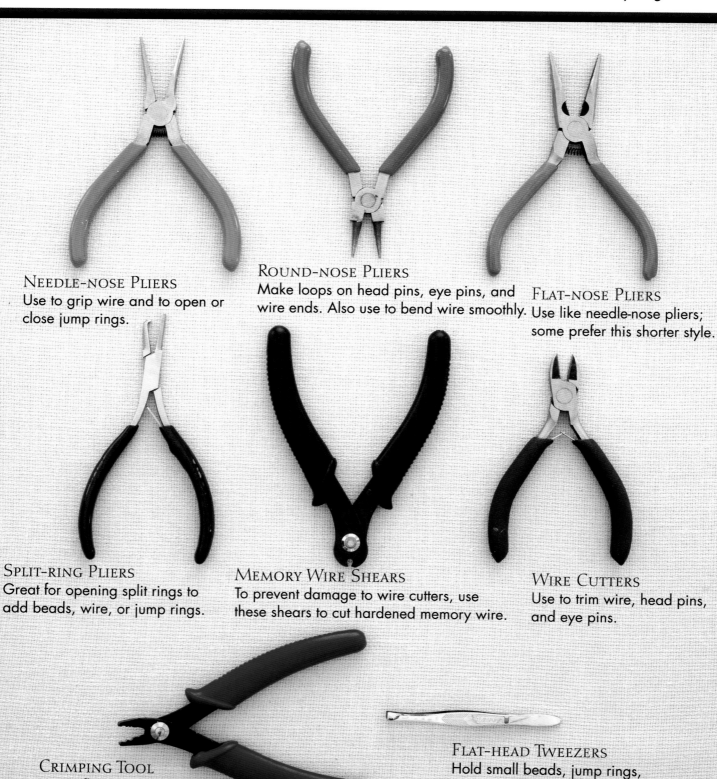

NEEDLE-NOSE PLIERS
Use to grip wire and to open or close jump rings.

ROUND-NOSE PLIERS
Make loops on head pins, eye pins, and wire ends. Also use to bend wire smoothly.

FLAT-NOSE PLIERS
Use like needle-nose pliers; some prefer this shorter style.

SPLIT-RING PLIERS
Great for opening split rings to add beads, wire, or jump rings.

MEMORY WIRE SHEARS
To prevent damage to wire cutters, use these shears to cut hardened memory wire.

WIRE CUTTERS
Use to trim wire, head pins, and eye pins.

CRIMPING TOOL
Use to flatten and bend crimp beads around wire.

FLAT-HEAD TWEEZERS
Hold small beads, jump rings, or chain links steady.

STRINGS & WIRES

Consider strength and style when choosing your stringing material, and be sure it fits through the beads.

STRETCH CORD
No clasps needed when using this stretchy plastic cord. It's great for bracelets and watches and more durable than thin elastic.

BEADING THREAD
Use with a beading needle to create jewelry with a soft, flowing design.

JEWELRY WIRE
This single-strand wire often comes on a spool. The higher the gauge, the thinner the wire.

COATED BEADING WIRE
This flexible wire is made of stainless steel strands coated with nylon. It is available in various diameters and strengths to accommodate different bead sizes and weights.

MEMORY WIRE
This hardened wire holds its shape and comes in pre-formed ring, toe ring, bracelet, and choker sizes.

TIGERTAIL
A good, inexpensive choice when strength is needed, tigertail is formed from strands of stainless steel wire coated with plastic or nylon.

LEATHER
Choose flat leather lace or round leather cord to enhance the natural beauty of your beads.

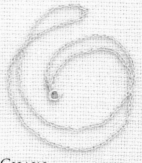

RIBBON
Add beads to ribbon for a delicate effect.

WAXED CORD
Available in many colors and sizes, waxed cord holds its shape well.

CHAIN
Add beaded dangles to an existing chain or intersperse chain pieces with beaded wire lengths to add interest to your design.

BEAD CHOICES

Beads come in a wide variety of materials and sizes. Choose a large bead, pendant, or charm as the focal bead in your design. Add medium-sized accent beads on each side and complete the piece with small beads, often spacers or seed beads, used as fillers.

Bone

Gemstone

Plastic

Metal

Pearl

Wood

Pressed Glass

Silver-lined E Bead

Lampwork Glass

Glass

Dichroic

Window

AB Finish

Ceramic

Shell

Bicone

Spacer

Beginning with the bicone beads on page 4, and continuing with the beads below, you'll see the abundance of bead shapes used in this book. Embellishments like pendants, charms, and buttons are also great design elements and add even more shape and texture to your jewelry.

Round

Flat Round

Cube

Teardrop

Tube

Seed

Bugle

Pony

Chip

Donut

Oval

Faceted

Pipe

Nugget

Pendant

Charm

Button

Jewelry Findings

Go from foundation to finale with connectors in between. See the Jewelry Findings Glossary on page 40 for more details.

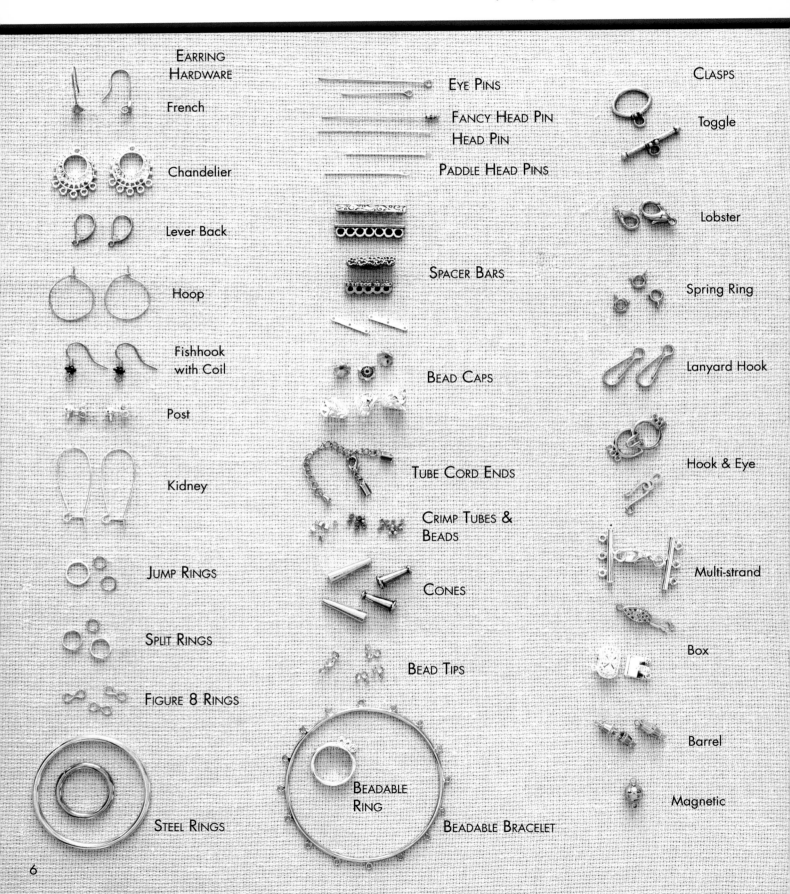

Earring Hardware
- French
- Chandelier
- Lever Back
- Hoop
- Fishhook with Coil
- Post
- Kidney

Jump Rings

Split Rings

Figure 8 Rings

Steel Rings

Eye Pins

Fancy Head Pin

Head Pin

Paddle Head Pins

Spacer Bars

Bead Caps

Tube Cord Ends

Crimp Tubes & Beads

Cones

Bead Tips

Beadable Ring

Beadable Bracelet

Clasps
- Toggle
- Lobster
- Spring Ring
- Lanyard Hook
- Hook & Eye
- Multi-strand
- Box
- Barrel
- Magnetic

SIZE IT UP
Guides for planning your designer jewelry.

COMMON BRACELET & NECKLACE LENGTHS
(Adjust the length of your project as desired.)

Bracelet	6" to 8"
Collar	12" to 13"
Choker	14" to 16"
Princess	17" to 19"
Matinee	20" to 24"
Opera	28" to 34"
Rope	40" to 45"
Lariat	Over 45"

APPROXIMATE BEADS PER INCH

Bead Size	1" Length
2mm	12.69
3mm	8.46
4mm	6.35
5mm	5.08
6mm	4.23
7mm	3.62
8mm	3.17
10mm	2.54
12mm	2.11
14mm	1.81
16mm	1.58
18mm	1.41
20mm	1.27

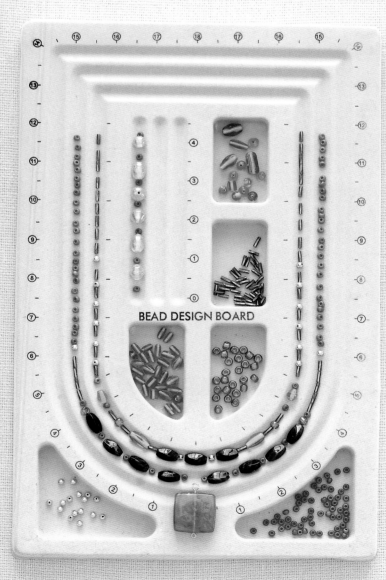

BEAD DESIGN BOARD

BEAD BOARD BASICS
A bead board makes it easy and fun to arrange your beads so you get that perfect look every time. Beginning in the center with a focal bead (if you have one) and working your way out, add accent, then filler beads to the outer channel of the board. Or, experiment with only one or two bead styles. Discover whether you want a repeating pattern or if you'd like a random design. Envision the look of multiple strands using the extra channels on the board. Play with one, two, or multi-colored bead families. Once you start, it's hard to stop, so measurements are marked on the board to remind you where to finish your beaded masterpiece.

MAKING CONNECTIONS   *Tips for holding it all together.*

ADDING CRIMP BEADS

To hold other beads in place, string a tiny crimp bead or crimp tube bead on the wire. Place the bead on the inner groove of the crimping tool and squeeze. Open the tool, turn the bead a quarter turn and place it in the outer groove of the tool. Squeeze to round out the crimp bead.

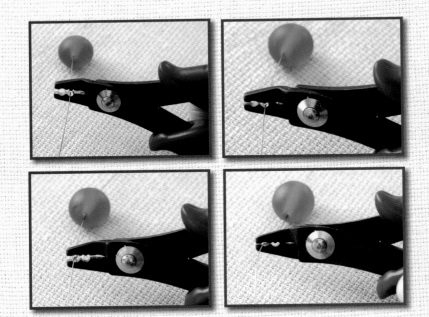

TYING KNOTS

Use an overhand knot with leather (shown), beading thread, cords, or ribbon. Tie a surgeon's knot when using waxed cord (shown), stretch cord, or beading thread. Add a drop of jeweler's cement or clear nail polish to the knot for extra strength.

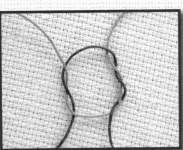

Connecting Strands to Clasps

For wire, thread a crimp bead and clasp on the wire end. Run the wire back through the crimp bead. Pull the wire tight; then, crimp the bead in place, and trim the wire end.

For waxed cord, string a bead tip on the cord and knot the end of the strand. Place the knot in the cup of the bead tip, trim the end, and close with needle-nose pliers. Attach the hook of the bead tip to a clasp or to a jump ring and clasp.

Opening & Closing Jump Rings

To keep this connecting ring from losing its shape, grasp the jump ring with two pairs of flat-nose pliers (one at each end of the opening). Pull one pair toward you while pushing the other away. Do the opposite to close.

Working with Split Rings

Since these rings are very strong, use split-ring pliers to simplify threading beads and wire loops onto the split ring.

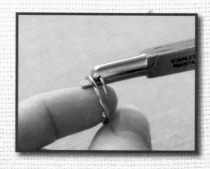

TECHNIQUES AT WORK
COLORFUL COMPOSITIONS

MONOCHROMATIC
Choose shades from one color family, creating a stunning design with different bead sizes, shapes, and arrangements. Metallic filler beads provide surprising highlights.

WARM & COOL TONES
Wire one bead color (or two neighboring colors) per strand. Combine all strands with decorative cones. Green, blue, and violet are calm cool colors and the lively warm colors consist of yellow, orange, and red.

Choosing bead combinations is exciting with all the fabulous colors and styles available. Here are some simple themes to think about when selecting the color palette for your design. Use the beaded color wheel on page 10 as a helpful guide.

COMPLEMENTARY COLORS

Choose color groupings from opposite sides of the color wheel (red & green, blue & orange, and yellow & violet are complementary colors). In this necklace, the violet color on each side of the tube-shaped focal bead finds its complement in the yellow beads closer to the clasp. Contrasting seed bead fillers round out the eye-catching design.

COLOR COUPLING

Alternate two bead colors, one dominant and one recessive, for an appealing duet (depending on the color of your outfit, the bead colors may switch in importance). Filler beads in a muted tone bring harmony to the piece.

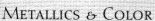

METALLICS & COLOR

Intersperse faceted glass beads with intricate metallic beads for a striking balance of color. Use silver metallics with cool-colored beads and combine gold metallics with warmer colors.

MULTIPLE STRANDS

Create multiple styles using multiple strands.

CRIMPED STRANDS WITH CONES

Crimp beads suspend larger beads in place on illusion-style wire strands. Run the wire ends on each side of the necklace through an eye pin and back through a crimp bead; crimp and trim. Insert the eye pin through the wide end of a cone; then, trim and loop the eye pin end at the top of the cone. Join the cone to a chain length with a jump ring.

PARTIAL STRANDS

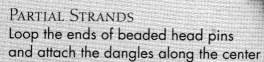

Loop the ends of beaded head pins and attach the dangles along the center of a chain necklace. Add beaded dangles to a shorter chain length and attach the ends to the necklace with jump rings.

SPACER BARS

Spacer bars added evenly throughout the design keep the strands separate and distinct from each other. To allow the choker to lie flat, use the least amount of beads on the inner strand and the most on the outer (our strands were 15", $16\frac{1}{2}$", and $18\frac{1}{2}$" long). Crimp the ends around jump rings attached to a three-strand hook & eye clasp.

KNOTTED STRANDS WITH CONES

String several strands on beading thread and knot the ends on each side of the necklace around the loop of an eye pin. Insert the eye pin through the wide end of a cone. Trim and loop the eye pin end at the top of the cone through the ring on the toggle clasp.

MULTI-STRAND END BARS

Taper your strands using smaller, more delicate beads at each end. Use crimp beads to attach the strands to multi-strand end bars; then, connect the bars to a lobster clasp with jump rings. To twist it up, take one end bar and insert it between the center strands near that end, then pull it through. Twist the strands as much as you like and clasp the ends.

SHAPING WIRE

Combine art and function using imagination and wires to accentuate your beads.

CURLED WIRE

CURLED WIRE PENDANT

Wire beads together in a freeform style. Twist a loop at the top to dangle the pendant from a cord, wire choker, or keychain. Finish each wire end with a beaded curl.

TWISTED WIRE FOB

String charms and beads on eye pins, head pins, and jewelry wire. Attach dangles to the fob's split ring with jump rings. Add jump rings between beads on the longest dangle; then, attach other dangles to the rings, twisting the wire ends tightly, loosely, and in between for a free and easy look.

TIGHTLY-TWISTED WIRE

LOOSELY-TWISTED WIRE

Wire loop

Curled Earrings with Wire Loop Dangles

Create ear wires from head pins for a custom design. Just clip off the heads and shape the wire as you wish (head pins are sturdy and will keep their shape well). Form a wire loop to add a beaded head pin dangle with single or multiple beads.

Coiled & Curled Brooch

String beads on two fancy head pins and thread one through one side of a buckle-shaped bead. Dip the pin in jeweler's cement and add a tube bead that fits in the buckle opening. Insert the other pin from the opposite side. Adding an artful component to the design, coil wire around the tube bead and curl the ends at the front of the brooch. Add more wire, a charm, and glue on a pin back.

Wrapped, Coiled, & Curled Bookmark

Start by wrapping heavy-gauge wire back and forth around your fingers. Add beads and tight wire coils where you wish. Curl up the ends for a fun finish. To add lightweight elements, thread beads on fancy head pins and twist the ends around coils on the bookmark.

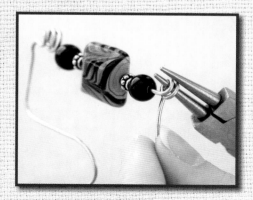

Coiled wire

BEADING PATTERNS

*Unleash your own jewelry style
with boundless pattern combos.*

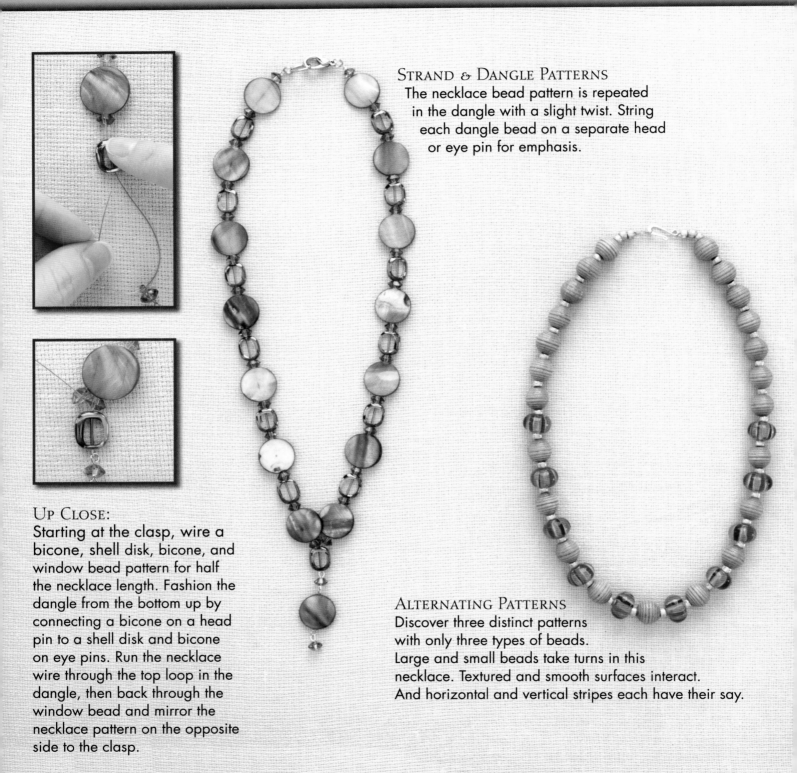

STRAND & DANGLE PATTERNS

The necklace bead pattern is repeated in the dangle with a slight twist. String each dangle bead on a separate head or eye pin for emphasis.

UP CLOSE:

Starting at the clasp, wire a bicone, shell disk, bicone, and window bead pattern for half the necklace length. Fashion the dangle from the bottom up by connecting a bicone on a head pin to a shell disk and bicone on eye pins. Run the necklace wire through the top loop in the dangle, then back through the window bead and mirror the necklace pattern on the opposite side to the clasp.

ALTERNATING PATTERNS

Discover three distinct patterns with only three types of beads. Large and small beads take turns in this necklace. Textured and smooth surfaces interact. And horizontal and vertical stripes each have their say.

STRAND PATTERNS
Beading wire is a strong silent partner in this design.

UP CLOSE:
String a split ring to the center of the wire and fold the wire in half. Thread a few beads on both strands; then, bead each strand separately for a bit. When you're ready, combine the strands and bead some more—back and forth as much as you like.

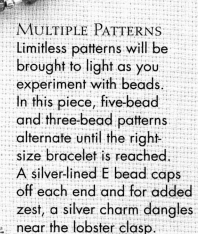

MULTIPLE PATTERNS
Limitless patterns will be brought to light as you experiment with beads. In this piece, five-bead and three-bead patterns alternate until the right-size bracelet is reached. A silver-lined E bead caps off each end and for added zest, a silver charm dangles near the lobster clasp.

FOCAL, ACCENT, & FILLER PATTERNS
A patterned focal grouping takes center stage on this necklace. It's flanked on either side by a pattern of accent beads, followed by a parade of sparkly filler beads interspersed with accent beads to maintain the continuity of the piece.

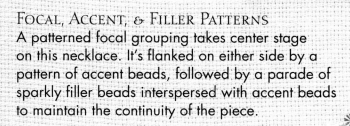

FOCAL POINTERS

Focal beads and charms make an even more noticeable statement when supported by unusual stringing materials.

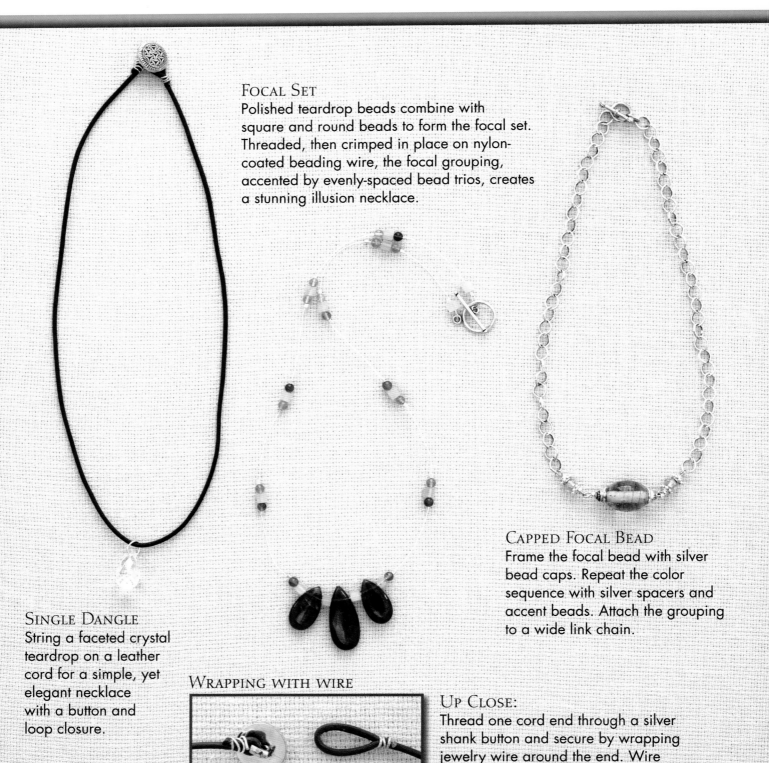

FOCAL SET
Polished teardrop beads combine with square and round beads to form the focal set. Threaded, then crimped in place on nylon-coated beading wire, the focal grouping, accented by evenly-spaced bead trios, creates a stunning illusion necklace.

CAPPED FOCAL BEAD
Frame the focal bead with silver bead caps. Repeat the color sequence with silver spacers and accent beads. Attach the grouping to a wide link chain.

SINGLE DANGLE
String a faceted crystal teardrop on a leather cord for a simple, yet elegant necklace with a button and loop closure.

WRAPPING WITH WIRE

UP CLOSE:
Thread one cord end through a silver shank button and secure by wrapping jewelry wire around the end. Wire a loop on the other end to create a unique clasp.

Detailed Dangle
Break up chain segments with intriguing beads and rings. Add an eye-catching focal charm and intricate dangles to bring harmony to the entire piece.

Framed Focal Bead
Knotted in place on silk ribbon, the curved glass focal bead is further accentuated by smaller metal and bicone beads on each side. The beaded ribbon ends tie on to a curb link chain that closes with a lanyard hook.

Focal Charm or Keepsake
Combine assorted chain lengths and styles with a beaded gemstone strand to make an asymmetrical backdrop for a treasured focal charm or keepsake. A round box clasp serves as an appealing closure to this design.

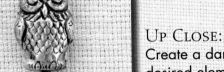

Up Close:
Create a dangle with desired elements from the necklace chain. Use jump rings to connect smaller charms that tie in with the focal charm. For a splash of color, add decorative head pins and eye pins threaded with coordinating beads.

DANGLES & PENDANTS

LOOPS & DANGLES

A simple chain becomes an unusual necklace with a few jump rings, eye pins, and glass beads. Join chain pieces to large jump rings with smaller rings. Thread beads onto eye pins and loop the straight end of each pin around a large ring. The bottom loop of each dangle reflects the overall look.

SINGLE PENDANT

Pick up the color scheme of your pendant with two shimmering strands of beads attached to a toggle clasp. Add a simple dangle near the clasp to highlight the central color of your necklace.

DANGLE EARRINGS

Thread a small metallic bead and a glass bead on a head pin. Connect the elegant dangle to a faceted oval channel bead for the perfect accent. Join to a lever back earring finding. Classic and quick.

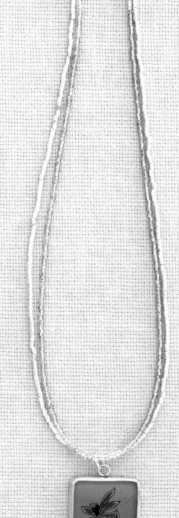

UP CLOSE:

Use a figure 8 ring to connect loops on the faceted channel bead to the lever back earring finding.

From graceful to playful, dangles and pendants are expressive components of your design.

BEAD PENDANT

Transform a large bead into a beautiful pendant using a head pin and two small beads. Loop onto a coordinating wire strand threaded with accent and filler beads.

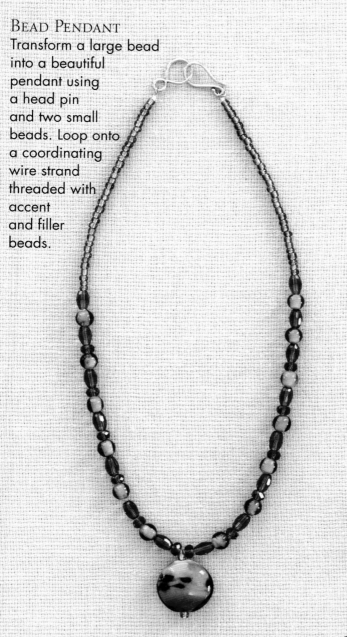

PENDANT & DANGLES

Combine jointed dangles with a distinctive pendant on oval chain links for a fun key fob. Thread beads on different head and eye pin lengths and include a charm to add character to the dangles.

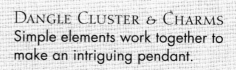

DANGLE CLUSTER & CHARMS

Simple elements work together to make an intriguing pendant.

UP CLOSE:

Add beads to eye pins and loop them onto a small jump ring. Attach the ring to a necklace chain. Connect some charms to another small ring. Knot embroidery floss and silk ribbon around a large jump ring and join it to each of the small rings.

1 BRACELET 3 WAYS

Add freeform dangles to a strand of beads to create an eclectic bracelet. Or for a classical arrangement, thread beads onto three strands of coated beading wire that run through a focal grouping, and crimp each strand to a multi-strand end bar. For a down-to-earth look, string beads on a single wire strand.

Diverse arrangements of the same essential beads give each bracelet its individual style.
The necklaces show variations on a basic theme with distinctive outcomes.

1 NECKLACE 3 WAYS

Join a pendant to a necklace chain. To add a bit of color,
cut the chain just above the dangle and add beaded eye pins.
To add still more color and a repeating pattern,
cut the chain in a few extra places and
include more beads.

THE RIGHT THREADS—Waxed cord lends a casual feel to a TEXTURED-BUTTON BRACELET. Wrap colored cord around steel rings and through wood tube beads to bind the elements of this NAPKIN RING. Waxed cord gives definition to the strands of the BEADED BRACELET with a button/loop closure and dangle. A CHOKER of leather cord and colorful beads commands attention. The dangles on this easy-to-spot KEY FOB are strung on double strands of beading thread.

DANGLING METALLICS

Coated beading wire holds together the perfect blend of metallics and color in the dangle BRACELET. Silver connector beads join lever back findings with beaded head pins for a striking EARRING SET. Smoky glass and metallic beads come together in clusters and dangles on this rollo chain NECKLACE.

Round it Out

Concoct WINE-GLASS CHARMS with earring hoops, crystal bicone beads, and inspiring oval word beads. Fasten a gemstone BRACELET with a magnetic clasp. Twist heavy wire into a RING and "sew" on beads and a button with fine wire. Connect beaded head pins to jump rings and add the multihued clusters to a BEADABLE BRACELET.

Mix it Up

The cool shades of a princess-length pendant NECKLACE are accented with silver rings and a fleur-de-lis charm. For a unique accessory, shape a MONOGRAM from armature wire and attach chip beads with fine jewelry wire. Engaging EARRINGS take shape from dichroic focal beads and glass bead accents on head pins that loop onto kidney-shaped ear wires. Multiple wired strands with simple beading patterns create an appealing two-tone BRACELET.

TEMPTING TREASURES—Tiny Japanese cylinder seed beads, nylon beading thread, and affirmation word pendants come together in a shimmering LARIAT NECKLACE. Form a wire RING with a loop at the top and add beaded head pins to your heart's content. To craft playful EARRINGS, join beaded head and eye pins to jump rings; then, wire the rings onto coiled fishhook ear wires via delicate bead caps. Turn a three-strand clasp into a six-strand BRACELET, by folding each length of beading wire in half; crimp and bead, adding AB finish faceted beads where you like.

PLEASING PATTERNS—The MEMORY WIRE BRACELET with beaded end dangles sports a cool monochromatic pattern based on bead size. Long beaded dangles on fancy head pins alternate with single-bead dangles to adorn CHANDELIER EARRINGS. Create a focal pattern NECKLACE on coated beading wire complete with accent and filler beads; simply attach to a chain with crimp beads. Several patterns blend to form this BRACELET of unusual beads and metallic button dangles secured with loosely-twisted wire loops.

SIMPLICITY—The loops on POST EARRINGS are meant for adding delicate glass beads on head pins. Thread clear, pearl, and shell beads on a two-strand stretch cord WATCHBAND. String buttons on stretch cord for a stylish BRACELET. To fashion a rope-length NECKLACE, tie knots in sheer ribbon to hold dichroic and metallic beads in place.

SPARKLE—Light dances on this graceful NECKLACE between the pewter cross and the faceted AB finish and tiny glass seed beads. A two-strand BRACELET mixes metallic charms, beads, and a chain with faceted crystal AB finish beads. For DAZZLING EARRINGS, thread faceted crystal AB finish beads on eye pins and fancy rose head pins; then, attach the dangles to French ear wires. Thread shiny wire-wrapped beads onto hoop ear wires for easy BREEZY EARRINGS.

GOLDEN TONES—The backdrop for a dramatic teardrop pendant NECKLACE is a three-color bead pattern strung on opera-length beading thread. Gold faceted AB beads are held in place with crimp beads on hoop EARRINGS. A glamorous RING is surprisingly shaped from beads and a glittering shank button on stretch cord. In this BRACELET, pearls and metallic beads on jewelry wire are crimped to the focal charm and toggle clasp.

WARM HUES—A three-strand CHOKER of round and rice-shaped beads is enhanced by a metallic charm with a red glass center. Decorate an adjustable RING with beaded head pins. Update an old watch face with a multi-strand beaded WATCHBAND, covering the band ends with jump rings and using a shank button and beaded loop for the clasp. A matinee-length NECKLACE shines with an appealing pattern of polished and textured beads on coated beading wire.

EYE CATCHERS—Attach beads, an upside-down watch (so the wearer can read it), and charms to a BROOCH. Metallic-colored beads, feather charms, and decorative jump rings hook up as impressive EARRINGS. Create a multi-strand NECKLACE, connecting decorative jump rings and beaded eye loops to a cut chain. Run two coated beading wires through an oval donut focal bead, adding round beads in the center; then, split the wires apart to bead the sides of the BRACELET. For each dangle EARRING, join two chain lengths to the loops of an eye pin running through the focal bead. Connect dangles to the bottom chain, then add a beaded chain and ear wire to the top chain.

ATTENTION GETTERS

A beaded wire WATCHBAND distinguishes its strands with spacer bars and a multi-strand box clasp. Make circular loops for dangle EARRINGS by threading beads on thin jewelry wire; then, crimp to secure each loop. A flat glass square bead and a printed metal pendant form a striking duo on this waxed linen NECKLACE with accent and filler beads tied in place.

METALLICS RULE—Jump rings attach charms and beaded head pins to a BRACELET chain. For custom-made chandelier EARRINGS, join dangles to triangles of silver-beaded eye pins. Wire an etched metallic shank button and donut bead to a single-loop RING. For a multi-strand NECKLACE, crimp two beaded strands onto eye pins, then thread through cones and connect to a chain.

POWER PLAY—Engaging EARRINGS combine dominant focal
teardrop beads on flat head pins with recessive medium-size accent
beads. Color coupling and multiple beading patterns culminate in a
chic princess-length NECKLACE. Repeat the beaded strand pattern
on both halves of the WATCHBAND, then add a bead-belly frog
charm on the wild side. Arrange a toggle BRACELET,
alternating muted coin and donut shell
beads with strong-colored glass beads.

TIMELESS TRINKETS

A silver tree pendant unites separate strands of brown and green beads with silver accents to form a tranquil NECKLACE. A faceted bead, slider, and charm swing and sway on a mini BOOKMARK. For a monogrammed BROOCH, glue a pin back to a stone bead, then add beaded strands and a focal charm. Reach for a fun and funky KEY FOB with beads and charms on an oversized chain.

CURRENT CLASSICS

Beads strung on elastic cord make a captivating NAPKIN RING. Clever and useful, a ribbon BOOKMARK is dressed up with beaded head pins and a spiral pendant. Attach an armature wire loop to a large donut bead and diverse dangles for a freeform TASSEL to hang from a drawer or doorknob. For a fresh and fringy BRACELET, loop beaded eye pins on a large link chain in a four-color repeating pattern.

JEWELRY FINDINGS GLOSSARY
from page 6

BEAD CAPS—Add texture and sparkle with metallic caps sized to fit the bead ends.

BEAD TIPS—Use to finish knotted strands; the cup on the bead tip hides the knot and the hook attaches to the ring or clasp.

BEADABLE BRACELET—Bracelet form with multiple loops for attaching beads, charms, or dangles.

BEADABLE RING—Ring form with one or more loops for attaching beads.

CRIMP TUBES & BEADS—Finish wire ends or hold beads in place as used in illusion-style jewelry.

CONES—Cover the ends of beaded strands with decorative cones that fit over beads.

EYE PINS, FANCY HEAD PINS, HEAD PINS, & PADDLE HEAD PINS—Use to add beaded dangles, make earrings, or connect chain links; available in assorted lengths.

FIGURE 8 RINGS—Enhance the design and function as connectors.

JUMP RINGS—Connect chain pieces or join lightweight dangles to a finding or chain.

SPACER BARS—Use to separate beaded strands; available in a variety of styles.

SPLIT RINGS—Excellent connectors for heavy dangles or chains.

STEEL RINGS—Use as jewelry connectors or pair them to make napkin rings.

TUBE CORD ENDS—To finish round leather cord, glue tube cord ends onto the leather and add a clasp with split rings.

TECHNIQUES INDEX